PATIENCE A[ ]ABI was bor[ ]
at Oxford [a]nd Sussex Universitie[s]. [R]enowned for her live
performanc[e]s, her poems have been broadcast on television
and radio all over the world. Her work has also appeared on
the London Underground and human skin. *Transformatrix* is her
second collection, the first being *R.A.W.* (Gecko Press, 1995).
She lectures in Creative Writing at the University of Kent and
lives in Gravesend.

TRANSFORMATRIX

PATIENCE AGBABI

CANONGATE

First published in 2000 by Payback Press,
an imprint of Canongate Books Ltd,
14 High Street, Edinburgh, EH1 1TE

10

The publishers gratefully acknowledge subsidy from the
Scottish Arts Council towards the publication of this volume

British Library Cataloguing-in-Publication Data
A catalogue record is available on request from the British Library

ISBN 978 0 86241 941 7

Typeset by Brian Young

Printed and bound by CPI Group (UK) Ltd, Croydon, CR0 4YY

www.canongate.tv

ACKNOWLEDGEMENTS

I would like to thank the following journals in which poems for this collection have appeared in some form: *Feminist Review* ('Martina', 'Ms De Meanour'), *Dummy* ('The Tiger'), *Calabash* ('Samantha'), *Poetry News* ('Who's Who?').

Some of these poems have also appeared in the following anthologies: *The Fire People* (Payback Press, 1998), *Bittersweet* (The Women's Press, 1998) and *IC3* (Penguin Books, 2000).

'69 BPM' was broadcast on *Love Thang*, BBC Radio 4, in 1996 and the 'Prologue' was broadcast as 'Word' on *The Essential Guide to the 21st Century*, BBC World Service, in 2000.

'Ufo Woman' was first cited on *Litpop*, Channel 4, in 1998. 'The Tiger' was broadcast on *The Other Side*, Channel 4, in 1999. 'If' was broadcast on *Culture Fix*, BBC Knowledge in 1999.

I would also like to thank the following friends and colleagues: Jamie Byng and Colin McLear for their enthusiasm and perseverance; Kwame Dawes for his inspiration and invaluable criticism; Steve Tasane for his regular creative feedback; Thea Bennett for her proofreading skills; Sarah Maguire for her encouragement; Carl St Hill aka Mo' Skills for his feminine rhymes; Samantha Coerbell for her sestinas; Melanie Abrahams for her excellent administrative and promotional skills; arts officers from Windhoek to Windsor for their hard work and love of poetry; and my family and friends for their constant love and support.

CONTENTS

PROLOGUE

Give me a word
any word
let it roll across your tongue
like a dolly mixture.
Open your lips
say it loud
let each syllable vibrate
like a transistor.
Say it again again again again again
till it's a tongue twister
till its meaning is in tatters
till its meaning equals sound
now write it down,
letter by letter
loop the loops
till you form a structure.
Do it again again again again again
till it's a word picture.
Does this inspire?
Is your consciousness on fire?
Then let me take you higher.

Give me a noun
give me a verb
and I'm in motion
cos I'm on a mission
to deliver information
so let me take you to the fifth dimension.
No fee, it's free,
you only gotta pay attention.
So sit back, relax,
let me take you back
to when you learnt to walk, talk,
learnt coordination
and communication,
mama
dada.
If you rub two words together you get friction
cut them in half, you get a fraction.
If you join two words you get multiplication.
My school of mathematics
equals verbal acrobatics
so let's make conversation.

Give me a preposition
give me an interjection
give me inspiration.
In the beginning was creation
I'm not scared of revelations
cos I've done my calculations.
I've got high hopes
on the tightrope,
I just keep talking.
I got more skills than I got melanin
I'm fired by adrenaline
if you wanna know what rhyme it is
it's feminine.
Cos I'm Eve on an Apple Mac
this is a rap attack
so rich in onomatopoeia
I'll take you higher than the ozone layer.
So give me Word for Windows
give me 'W' times three
cos I'm on a mission
to deliver information
that is gravity defying
and I'll keep on trying
till you lose your fear of flying.

Give me a pronoun
give me a verb
and I'm living in syntax.
You only need two words to form a sentence.
I am I am I am I am I am
bicultural and sometimes clinical,
my mother fed me rhymes through the umbilical,
I was born waxing lyrical.
I was raised on Watch with Mother
The Rime of the Ancient Mariner
and Fight the Power.
Now I have the perfect tutor
in my postmodern suitor,
I'm in love with my computer.
But let me shut down
before I touch down.

Give me a word
give me a big word
let me manifest
express in excess
the M I X
of my voice box.
Now I've eaten the apple
I'm more subtle than a snake is.
I wanna do poetic things in poetic places.
Give me poetry unplugged
so I can counter silence.
Give me my poetic licence

and I'll give you metaphors that top eclipses
I'll give megabytes and megamixes.

Give me a stage and I'll cut form on it
give me a page and I'll perform on it.

Give me a word
any word.

HIGH-FLYING FEMMES

UFO WOMAN (PRONOUNCED OOFOE)

I

Mother Earth. Heath Row. Terminal 5. Yo!
Do I look hip in my space-hopper-green
slingbacks, iridescent sky-blue-pink skin
pants and hologram hair cut? Can I have
my clothes back when you've finished with them, please?
Hello! I just got offa the space ship.

I've learnt the language, read the VDU
and watched the video twice. Mother Earth
do *you* read *me*? Why then stamp my passport
ALIEN at Heath Row? Did I come third
in the World Race? Does my iridescent
sky-blue-pink skin embarrass you, mother?

LONDON. Meandering the streets paved with
hopscotch and butterscotch, kids with crystal
cut ice-cream cones and tin-can eyes ask 'Why
don't U F O back to your own planet?'
Streets paved with NF (no fun) graffiti
Nefertiti go home from the old days.

II

So I take a tram, tube, train, taxi trip
hip-hugged, bell-bottomed and thick-lipped, landing
in a crazy crazy cow pat. SUSSEX.
Possibly it's my Day-Glo afro, rich
as a child paints a tree in full foliage
that makes them stare with flying saucer eyes.

Perhaps my antennae plaits in winter
naked twigs cocooned in thread for bigger
better hair make them dare to ask to touch.
'*Can we touch your hair?*' Or not ask at all;
my two-tone hand with its translucent palm,
life line, heart line, head line, children, journeys,

prompting the *'Why's it white on the inside
of your hand?' 'Do you wash? Does it wash off?'*
Or my core names, Trochaic, Dactylic,
Galactic beats from ancient poetry,
names they make me repeat, make them call me
those sticks-and-stones-may-break-my-bones-but names.

In times of need I ask the oracle.
Withdrawing to my work station I press
HELP. I have just two options. HISTORY:
The screen flashes subliminal visuals
from the old days which I quickly translate:
Slave ship: space ship, racism: spacism.

Resignedly I select HERSTORY:
The screen displays a symmetrical tree
which has identical roots and branches.
I can no longer reason, only feel
not aloneness but oneness. I decide
to physically process this data.

III

So I take the train plane to the Equator
the Motherland, travel 5 degrees North
to the GO SLOW quick-talking fast-living
finger-licking city known as LAGOS.
Streets paved with gold-threaded gold-extensioned
women and silk-suited men; market-stalls

of red, orange, yellow and indigo.
Perhaps it's not my bold wild skin colour,
well camouflaged in this spectrum of life,
but the way I wear my skin, too uptight,
too did-I-wear-the-right-outfit-today,
too I-just-got-off-the-last-London-flight;

or my shy intergalactic lingo
my monospeak, my verbal vertigo
that makes them stare with flying saucer eyes.
They call me Ufo Woman, oyinbo
from the old days which translates as weirdo,
white, outsider, other, and I withdraw

into myself, no psychedelic shield,
no chameleonic facade, just raw.
Then I process Ufo and U F O,
realise the former is a blessing:
the latter a curse. I rename myself
Ufo Woman and touch base at Heath Row.

IV

No. Don't bother to strip, drug, bomb search me
I'm not staying this time. Why press rewind?
Why wait for First World *Homo sapiens*
to cease their retroactive spacism?
Their world may be a place worth fighting for
I suggest in the next millennium.

So, smart casual, I prepare for lift off,
in my fibre-optic firefly Levis,
my sci-fi hi-fi playing *Revelations*
and my intergalactic mobile ON.
Call me. I'll be surfing the galaxy
searching for that perfect destination.

THE JOYRIDER

I'm a dangerous driver at a dead end
the wrong way up a one-way
knuckles rigid with road rage,
stripped raw in a single cell,
in the damp womb of the Women's Wing.
They called it a clear-cut case:
Speeding, Possession, Resisting Arrest,
TDA and Drink Driving.
Wheel-clamped, my car keys
were flushed down the wishing well.
So I'm inside, soul searching,
fallen woman at a white wedding,
rough ruby on a diamond ring.
    I miss meeting up with my mates,
wicked weekends on Es and whizz
fast food and the free flow
of Dormobiles and double-deckers
Land Rovers, Range Rovers,
XR2s and XR3s,
horns hooting like hecklers.
Give me sunshine, four-star,
the clunk-click of a stolen car
and I'm wicked witch of the wheel,
swapped my broomstick for a gearstick.
    I'm fisting the future, flying
high in a Hot Hatchback
in my bright pink pedal-pushers
and my two-tone trainers.
Ask anyone, easy as CBA.
The roundabout and ring-road
whizz by, the windscreen wipers
waving like weekend ravers
and I'm tight turning for a tune,
heading for Hip Hop.
Mad Maxine on amphetamine,
I live for the finishing line,
the time-travel of tarmac,
the runway of the M1.
Forcing my foot through the floor,
inhaling the fast lane,
I hit fifth. A hitch hiker
blurs by. The boom of the bass.

And Adam's apple meets Armageddon,
I just reached the junction for joy.
      They found speed in the cell search,
pink wraps in my powder puff.
I'm sleepwalking in a single cell
manics and valium don't mix.
I'm palpitating on kangaroo petrol.
I want my mum, I miss her so much.
The women here are hard as hell,
back-seat drivers or diesel dykes.
It's break free or breakdown.
I hate the cycle, the cold, clammy
timetable of tea and tranqs.
Time travels slow doing time.
      They arrive like a racing rival,
lights, sirens, 666.
It hits home at a hundred:
either brave the odds, break the barrier
or slow down, stop, surrender.
The devil or death by speeding.
I hit the clutch, change conscience
and catch sight of my stiff sentence
bold as a Belisha beacon.
      Why should I suffer in silence?
I never caused a car crash
never had a hit-and-run
never hurt no-one.
Just born bad, petrol for blood.
I ram raid man-made rules,
accelerate into the sunset.

THAT FOUR FOUR TRIP

Tabs. Acid tabs. Acid tabs four quid.
Tabs. Acid tabs. Acid tabs four quid.
Tabs. Acid tabs. Acid tabs four quid.
Tabs. Acid tabs. Acid tabs four quid.

"Hear that, Jill? Want some acid?" asks Jack, acid head, cool dude, mine.

"Yeah, sure".

Tabs. Acid tabs. Acid tabs four quid...

"Only four quid, mate," says blue eyed drug boss.

Jack gets four. Pays hard cash. I'll drop, Jack will drop like it's play time. Time will melt down into four four beat. Rock, jazz, rave. This year it's more busy, more wild. Soon that drug rush will come, that acid kick. Open your mind wide open. Trip.

Rave tent. Full. Arms, legs pump, pump, pump, pump. Jack, Sara, 2000 kids into that tune, that beat, that deep, sexy, rock hard bass. It's that tune from last year, same tent, same time, when Jack came over with some acid tabs. 'Open wide,' he'd said. Then we'd made love, till dawn, till dusk. It's that same tune. It's ours.

Does Sara look like Kate Moss? Yeah. Shit. I've full hips, huge tits. Jack says he's into thin, into free love when he's high. I've gone wild with envy. Feel huge. It's this trip. I've slid down into trip hell. Help. Need help. Need beer. Yeah. Plus junk food. I'll diet next week. I'll walk east into this city, find some grub, come back.

"Jack!"

"What?"

"Need fuel. I'll come back soon. Want some beer?"

"Yeah! Sara will want some. Grab four cans."

Sara just took some acid. Burn baby burn. I'll come back when this meal goes down.

Full moon. What does full moon mean? Lost city goes gaga. I've gone gaga. I've just left Jack with sexy Sara. Find main drag. Beer tent very busy. Some boys sell beer from Nike bags. Each coin will turn into cans. XXXX. Open wide. It's very cold, very very good. Need food. Here they only sell cake. Dope cake. I'll find that chip shop that does meat pies. Feet ache. I'll walk slow. Will fall down very soon. Must find food.

Must find tent. Tent city? More like toon town. East runs into west. I've lost tent. Pale blue. Dark blue? Grey? Lost this tiny

mind. It's huge like this city, each road, each path, each tree. Free your mind from that head cage. Tear that quad into four tiny tabs. Each take your acid with love. Find your self. Solo. High. Like lady moon. Each trip will link.

Pink neon sign says home. Jack tied pink flag onto tent pole. Hero! It's cold, damp. Safe. This hour I'll wind down. Only *this* time fate will play iron lady. I'll hear that same tune, that same four four beat. Soon I'll feel eyes, nose, ears, lips turn warm. This face will slip down like silk. This body will lose form. Each limb will melt onto tent base, flow like acid wine, iron flat, form into quad. Soon I'll turn into acid.

When body dies, mind must take over. I've just died. Just like that. Gone into next life. Feel even more gaga than last time. Good news: I've come back very slim. Roll over Kate Moss. Evil news: I've lost arms, legs plus feet. Only this very very tiny body left over, just this thin quad card body. Just this face with wide eyes.

Acid tabs were kids once, kids that flew mega high then fell into this cage, this trap. They only have life when some cool dude eats them. Acid tabs need some mind they must fuck with.

"Jill! It's Jack. I've come home."

He's with Sara. Hear zips, more zips, then Jack puts head into tent door.

"Jill must have gone. Come here, love."

Love! Shit face. Your love just grew cold. Very cold. Hear them kiss. Arse hole! Each kiss will turn into love bite. Each bite will hurt like acid pain. He's mine, Sara. Some acid tabs look good, some acid tabs look evil. I'll look good. Free acid! Over here, Jack, over here. Will they make love? Over this dead body. Fuck them.

Then iron lady fate does back flip. Jack sees Miss Acid Face.

"Well, well, well. Look, Sara!"

"Yeah, more acid."

"That face!"

"What face?"

"Look. It's like Jill, only it's ..."

"Thin?"

Wait till I've come down. I'll slap your smug, baby doll face, Sara, till it's pulp.

"Sara, take half."

Half! Help. I've only this tiny self left.

"Jack. I've gone cold. Must rest. It's your trip, baby."

"Sure?"

"Yeah."

Open wide Jack. Lick your lips, bite this thug baby, hold onto your mind. I've gone deep down into your body. It's warm, dark down here. Hear your drum beat, your bass line, your four four. It's that same tune. I'll keep time with that, hold onto that. I've gone down into that tube shit goes. Soon I'll turn into shit, your shit. Then I'll come back, shit face.

I've gone deep down into your sick mind, your hard disk. Each file says 'fuck'. I'll fuck. I'll fuck with your head, head, head, head. Your mind will link with mine, mine, mine, mine. I'll make love with your fear. I'll make your dick hard, iron hard like fate. Sara will like that. Then when it's mega good, I'll make your dick soft, limp, tiny, more tiny, even more tiny, like some worm, thin, gone, gone, gone.

"Holy shit!"

Well, Jack. Take acid, take that risk. Look back over your life, your long long trip. Drug life, nine: love life, zero. Take your time. D'ya hear that tune, dude? D'ya hear that four four beat? It's that same tune from last year, this year, next year, bass that ties body with soul, Jack with Jill. It's ours, Jack. Only Jill will make your deep, sexy, rock hard bass come back.

It's nice here. Like some warm, safe womb. I'll stay till dawn, take this mind down some slip road. Sara will have gone. Jack will shit then, shit this body back, cast away this evil twin mind. I'll come back, come down with warm beer, dope cake, fags. Jack will trip till noon, till dusk, till that bass hits like mega boom from hell, till arms, legs, head grow warm, burn, melt down.

22

BUFFALOS AND SILVER STILETTOS

There's this boy, right. Well, he's nineteen and his name's Shane and he's just moved into number thirty-nine. I know all this cos my mate Sonya got accidentally-on-purpose chatting to his mum and reported back in double maths. And I got told off for talking cos I had to repeat everything twice cos I've got this new brace, d'ya get me, and I'm not taking the piss but it makes me speak like thith.

I've started leaving early for school. As soon as he passes the estate, I throw on my Buffalos and follow him all the way to Seven Sisters. He works in Pizza Hut, Walthamstow. My mum fancies him as well cos she's started going to Tesco really early like there was a food shortage but there's never any more food in the fridge.

Anyway, they're having this house-warming and invited Sonya and Sonya's invited me and mum and some other friends, well the whole street from number 1 to number one million. Believe! And I'm borrowing mum's silver stilettos though she's a four and I'm a five and I'll probably do a nose-dive right in front of Shane and he'll end up getting off with that butters Charmaine.

Now I've done my hair and my nails and I'm really buff if I don't smile and my dress is so tight I can't sit down. So I get to practice walking in the heels. These shoes are ill. They're not that tight. And Sonya says that all the catwalk girls are wearing these stilettos. Still, when I leave, I can't help noticing my Buffalos.

I love their flat. It's painted blue and green and I wish I lived somewhere like that. But the vibe's dry, d'ya get me. Like the whole family flew over from Jamaica and they're playing reggae singles! Ain't they heard of jungle? There's three women walking round with these bowls of peanuts and pistachios an' I feel like I'm walking on hot coals.

So I'm standing in the kitchen with my plate of chicken and my rum punch trying not to look like I'm crippled when guess who comes through the door? Believe! I'm staring at the pattern in the wallpaper when he comes over. He looks like he's gonna ask me to dance. He clears his throat and says, "Are you one of my Jamaican aunts?"

While I'm choking on my drink, he says he was joking but I'm already thinking in the light of the kitchen he's not that good-looking. Still, he tells me there's a rave out East, there's a group of them going. And you know what they say about plenty more fish in the sea. But he does have style so I have to smile even though it looks like barbed wire. Then he grins back, says he likes my footwear, an' you know what? It feels like I'm walking on air.

DEVILS IN RED DRESSES

THE EXCORIATION

I

For my twelfth birthday I asked for a snake,
green, white and green. I fed it raw whitebait

and named it Hope after my best friend Hope
who sends me thin blue letters from Lagos.

That night my father dined on raw silence
but my dreams were embossed with his curses

translated through rose-pink anaglypta.
That grave morning after, my stepmother,

tired and white, whispered me the bad news
as I smirked behind striped brushed cotton sheets.

Hope was donated to the local zoo
and I was expelled from home to boarding school.

II

I am getting too big for my body.
Tiny fists for breasts. Bomb-black thighs. Silence
plucks each brazen swelling. I'm a ripe bruise

smarting under double-barrelled asides.
I bleed letters to Queen's College, Lagos,
stilted in pidgin English and I bleed

pink-black humiliation as Miss strips
my vowels, clips my consonants until
my voice breaks in Queen's English. The puce scar

is bleached blonde on stiff white cotton gusset,
an invisible message for mummy
who forgives me at half-term, pink and smiling.

III

For my thirteenth birthday I've asked for a horse.

THE WIFE OF BAFA

My name is Mrs Alice Ebi Bafa
I come from Nigeria.
I am very fine, isn't it.
My next birthday I'll be twenty-nine.
I'm business woman.
Would you like to buy some cloth?
I have all the latest styles from Lagos,
Italian shoe and handbag to match,
lace, linen and Dutch wax.
I only buy the best
and I travel first class.
    Some say I have blood on my hands
'cause I like to paint my nails red
but others call me femme fatale.
My father had four wives
so I've had five husbands.
I cast a spell with my gap-toothed smile
and my bottom power.
Three were good and two were bad.
    The first three were old and rich
and I was young and fit.
They died of exhaustion.
The fourth one was ladies' man.
I could not count his women on one hand
but he'd rage if I looked at another man.
I was very wild when I was young.
They called me Miss Highlife,
I was not considered a good wife
but I always respected my husband.
He died when I returned from this London.
    The last one I married for love.
He was studying law at University of Ibadon.
He was not yet twenty-one,
wicked in bed and so handsome
but he liked pornographic magazine.
His favourite was *Playboy*.
One day I threw it on fire
to teach him a lesson.
He turned into wife batterer.
He was to regret his action.
I beat him till he screamed for his ancestors.
Now we get on like house on fire.

Some say I'm a witchcraft
'cause I did not bear them children.
They do not understand your Western medicine.
    You like my headtie.
It's the latest fashion.
They sell like hot cake on Victoria Island.
Fifty pounds.
I give you discount 'cause I like your smile.
The quality is very good.
If I take off more I will not make profit.
I travel to Lagos next week.
Make it my lucky day.
Please, I beg you.

THE HEADDRESS

I meet a bird with a double-barrelled name
at some party. Next thing I know, I'm at Ascot
with the nobs. Horses all look the same
to me, Red Rum, Roll-a-joint. I'm not

a gambling man, myself but I put a few quid
down on the favourite and it comes in,
so I put down fifty on an outsider and I kid
you not, I pull in two grand on that win.

So, I'm the dog's bollocks now, 'scuse my French
and get talking to a couple of diplomats
and order some champagne, something to quench
our thirst. Then I start checking out the hats.

Now I'm a hips man, myself, make no mistake.
I like my women with hips like horses
but there's nothing like a broad hat and a bit of fake
fruit on top to make a man divorce his

principles. She's standing by the bar
like one of those statues carved out of ebony.
If she was a dish, she'd be caviar.
She's a black widow weaving her web on me

turning your common or garden thread into gold.
In the midst of all this money, she's true class.
She doesn't need make-up in order to get dolled
up and she's got this spectacularly huge glass

of brandy in her hand. But I'm looking at her hat,
a straw hat topped with fake fruit. I can tell it
cost an arm and a leg. More fruit than you can shake a stick at:
a pineapple so lifelike I can almost smell it,

a tangerine, a mandarin, an orange,
a peach, a pear, a plum, a bunch of black grapes,
and a watermelon. And you know what? I'm ready to binge,
getting off on all these colours and shapes.

Well, what can I do but ask her if she wants a drink.
Would she care for a Brandy Alexander? Yes.
So I empty the champagne into her glass and we clink:
here's to Jack the lad and the African goddess.

She tells me her Western name's Ellen
and in between cocktails manages to sell
the pineapple, the bunch of grapes and the watermelon
to Mr and Mrs dirty weekend in posh hotel.

I tell her she can call me Paddy or Patrick.
She turns her head, her basket of fruit, to smile.
At Lord's, you'd call it a hat trick,
at Ascot, pure style.

BITCH

I'm camera shy,
never starred in the school play,
never looked fear in the eye
till today.

She'd said "Harry, baby,"
she said "Please," she said
"Do it if you love me."
There's a firing squad

of TV cameras
stalking my every move.
I feel sick, ugly, impotent as
unrequited love

and she's smiling
vampire red as she's saying it,
squeezing my hand, "Darling,
you know I love you so much but

I'm having an affair."
My watch stops ticking.
I'm looking straight at her
and all I'm seeing is her fucking

my best mate
but I'm the one who's sweating
till love congeals to hate
till every pore is hating

her, hating him
and the slow burning
humiliation, the crimson.
I can hear a bucket creaking

overhead, hear it swinging
like in *Carrie*
and the audience laughing
and her pleading, "Harry,

say something, baby,"
and all I can do is croak
"How could you do this to me?"
Then I'm spitting pure rage, "It's Dick,

isn't it." But she lowers
her gold-shadowed eyelids,
"No," she pauses for what seems like hours
inhales, and opens her lips, "It's

Rex."
I wish I could just press a button, switch
channels. I've just gone off sex.
The only word that passes the censors is "Bitch".

They bring him in on a lead.
The crowd scream.
He's tugging at the leash, she's stroking his head
and she's kissing him.

Whoever thought up the phrase
'man's best friend',
whoever felt love like a bruise
will understand

why I hit that hellhound,
as if nobody else was there
except me and him and my girlfriend
till they carried me back to my chair.

R & B

Put on your red dress, baby,
let me button up my blue jeans.
You revitalize me daily,
you're the life-blood running through my veins.

You're the setting sun in my clear, blue sky
and in my midnight-blue you're the harvest moon.
Sometimes we argue and I don't know why,
you're Mars and I'm Neptune.

You accuse me of quenching your fire:
I accuse you of blocking my flow
but you're the ruby to my sapphire,
you're the bright red cherry to my blue-black sloe.

You're the red rag to my raging bull.
You always see red when I sing the blues.
You're the ladybird tracing the ridge of my clavicle.
You're the lipstick on my collar, I'm your blue suede shoes.

You're the redbreast on my blue velvet.
I'm the aerogramme in your postbox.
You're my ruby slippers, you're my red carpet.
I'm the poet but baby, you're my thought-fox.

You're the red in enamoured, you're wicked.
You're Scarlett O'Hara, I'm Betty Blue.
I'm the blue pill in *The Matrix* and you're the red.
You're my red phone bill, overdue.

You've got more kick than red rum,
you're red raw, red-handed, red-hot.
I metamorphose into blue nun.
You're love-lies-bleeding, I'm forget-me-not.

You say we were a mismatched couple
but I'm reminiscing too.
I remember how we made the colour purple
and my eyes are red from missing you.

POPPIES AND FRESH RED RIBBONS

I

Arthur is remembering
Joe speaking blood. He's singing
hymn number one in silence
resonant as shell shock. "Once
you kill a man, you kill twice:
war's intimate sacrifice ...
the living mimic the dead."
Memories of Joe's naked
torso, proud as a tree trunk,
the private he left punch-drunk
and the hot hit of his sweat,
their arms locked in mock combat.
Arthur has loved without him
almost sixty years. Women
press his clothes. His uniform
is starched with memory. Warm
firm hands shake his, some shaking.
The congregation rise, sing
remembrance. Then men embrace
their sixty seconds of peace.

II

Sixty beats-per-minute peace
resounds love. Then men embrace.
The diamond diva sings
Adam's apple-pip-shaking
soprano. It's sunny, warm.
Duke eyes men in uniform
but idolizes women
who launder gossip for him.
In black Calvins and combats,
pierced lips, locks angry with sweat,
Duke waves up to the punch-drunk
air, John, bronze in silver trunks,
diving. But the sky's naked,
featureless blue and John's dead.
Duke dreads his own sacrifice,
life, for John's gap-toothed smile. Twice
he's tasted its spittle. Once
on their first night when silence
framed their fate, caged birds singing.
The last, he's remembering.

SEVEN SISTERS

MARTINA

I must have been sweet sixteen at the time,
boyish, straight up straight down. She was the girl
next door but one, living at the dark end
of the street, the fat ugly duckling child
who grew up gorgeous. A different boy
for each day of the week. She was a dark

horse, kept herself to herself, her sloe-dark
eyes revealing nothing. It was wartime
and rations chiselled our features but boy,
she kept her curves. I was a grown-up girl,
she was woman. Time had silenced the child
in her eyes. We prayed for the war to end

in our Sunday best. But we were weekend
disciples, evacuees scared of dark
nights pierced with blitzkrieg pyrotechnics, child-
like, clinging to mother's skirt. She found time
to party in new nylons, good-time girl
growing voluptuous from man and boy,

on chocolate and plum brandy. I was tomboy
running errands, climbing trees till the end.
But she was the midnight-rouge glamour girl
who French-kissed GI lovers in the dark
who drawled, "Anytime, lady, anytime."
She was wicked woman: I was wild child.

We all knew she was expecting a child.
In those days we all expected the boy
to marry her. But, it being wartime,
too soon his two-month leave came to an end.
Her father threw her out into pitch-dark
November's clutches with the words "No girl

of mine ..." She gave birth to a baby girl,
Martina. They wanted to put the child
up for adoption. Tina had the dark
features of her father, the soldier boy
tortured by fate's keen bullet till the end,
bleeding dry on a battlefield. In time,

she got married for the child's sake, a boy-
next-door type; and in time I met a girl
with sloe-dark eyes and loved her till the end.

THE TIME TRAVELLER

Fasten your seat belts. We're now entering a new time
zone. It's six hours to New York. I'm their GMT-girl,
I wouldn't recommend the food. *Weekend
break, madam? (Rich bitch).* We're getting rather child-
ish in the aisles, frolicking like choirboys.
I like take-off best. Ruby-, topaz-, emerald-stabbing dark,

the roar of the engine, the earth arching its peat-dark
spine. I'm learning to tell the time
in fifteen different languages to buoy
up my CV. I've got a Russian degree and I was cover girl
for *Time Out* in 1988. *Would your child
like vegetarian (dog shit) too, sir?* At the end

of this shift I'll be 30. I'll celebrate the butt-end
of the decade in New York in the dark
with pink candles, a bloated child
in a white satin bow, extinguishing time.
Five hours behind but light years ahead for a girl
into triple-decker sandwiches and toy boys.

I guess I prefer sandwiches to toy boys
and paper plates to paper planes. This weekend
it'll be cake, champagne and ... *Has your little girl
really been gone fifteen minutes? (tempus fugit)* ... dark
rye bread topped with rollmop herring ... *The Times?
Sorry, we only have* The Express. *The child?*

*No, she's not upstairs. How old is your child,
madam? Thirteen? (Then she's probably shagging some boy
in the loos).* As I was saying, herring, pickle and a prime-time
soap to wash it all down. All good dreams must end
in New York. The bright stitch of city lights, the dark
ticking of rain. And I'm the porcelain T-girl,

the bone-china babe. *Strap in your little girl
after yourself, sir. (Would the hysterical screaming child
like a breath of fresh air?)* Everything's tomb-dark
for landing. *Clunk click, madam (The life buoy's
under your seat but nothing'll save you in the end.
When you die, you die, there's never a perfect time.)*

Have a nice weekend. Enjoy your time
in New York, girls and boys. Has someone lost a dark
brown patent-leather Gucci glove? Has anyone found a child?

THE EARTH MOTHER

Once upon a time
there lived a wise old woman and a young girl,
one at the beginning, the other at the end
of ripeness but Old Woman craved another child
to chop the wood and mend the roof, a boy
whose skin would sing the tone of potent dark.

She waited for the forest to bleed dark
then ordered Girl to gather lavender, wild thyme,
frogs' legs, a snail's antennae and the special Boy
ingredient: the skinned tail of an Alsatian pup. Girl
set off but being a short-sighted child,
mistook a glow-worm for a dog's tail end.

That weekend
Old Woman made the pottage in her womb-dark
cauldron, and she drank, and was with child.
And autumn came and winter went and springtime
lit the black earth with snowdrops. Girl
conversed with snakes and conquered trees while Boy

grew thumbs and learnt to suck them both. Soon Boy
grew restless and Old Woman knew her term must end.
"Look in the convex mirror of my belly, Girl.
Translate to light that which is dark,"
and Girl replied "It's time!"
The forest heaved and wept. The child

was slow to leave its mother, a king-size child
black as a juniper berry. Old Woman named it Boy
and dreamt earth, wind and fire, better times ...
And here the tale would end
if little girls could truly tame the dark
and little boys were really boys, not girls.

Old Woman woke and saw her baby Boy was girl
and being wise, gave praise and raised this girl-child
to chop the wood and mend the roof. By dark
the three would eat hot pottage, Girl and Boy
sat side by side, Old Woman at the end
remembering the time,

that first weekend, when the pot bubbled wild thyme
and a child lit up the dark
bowl of her belly, the girl-child she named Boy.

MS DE MEANOUR

It's midnight. Party time.
Time for a girl
to hit the West End
so hard it shrieks like a child,
lover boy.
Don't you just adore the dark,

the funky smell of the dark?
Midnight chimes. Time
for boy
meets girl
in the mirror and wild child
bitch with a dick from Crouch End

becomes Wild West End
diva with dark
luscious lashes, courtesy of every child's
dream fairy godmother. Time
to lose the glass slipper, Cinderella. Diamonds are a girl's
best friend and boy

oh boy,
I'm harder than a brickie from Mile End!
A girl's gotta do what a girl's
gotta do. Strap it in before the pumpkin carriage beeps its dark
bulbous time-
to-hit-the-road horn. Now I'm a child,

the bastard child
of Barbara Cartland and Boy
George, in a sequinned shift, checking the time
on a Rolex. I hear the wheels scrape the end
of the street and I dive into the dark.
Go girl!

Strut your funky stuff, girl!
Cos the night's a hyperactive child
on E129 and the dark
is every boy's
sheath. West End
is where it's at and it's party time.

Let the wild child
burn the wick at both ends
cos the time is ripe for girls who are boys in the dark.

THE TIGER

LOVE HATE in black and blue, the first time.
Miss Carter wrote "Tracy is a very bright girl
but she plays the fool like a veteran."
        That weekend
I tasted salt-sweet lust and lost my child-
hood somewhere along the beach. The boy
was Darren Smith. It was damp-dark,
hairs-standing-on-end dark.
I wore a black polo neck for weeks.
        The next time
was the last day of school when some boy
scrawled *SLAG* on my graffitied blouse and my girl-
friend scribbled it into an ugly scar. The first child
to abandon school, I marched to the end
of the pier, the bleach-blonde end
of an era, wishing for the anonymity of dark.
And later I rolled up my sleeve like a child
giving blood for the first time.
Tracy loves Darren. It was girl
power, 1979. He was my aerosol boy
and the swelling inscription, my lifebuoy.
We lasted a month.
       The next time was Southend,
1980. The receptionist was Tank Girl,
the tattooist, Cruella De Ville, who stitched hot, dark
ink into my taut flesh as time
flowed free in a corset of glass. I was a child
bride, married to the needle and our child
was the fine-line distinction, like girl, boy,
the miracle of living flesh. Time
was exquisite subcutaneous pain and the end
marked the beginning, a jet-dark,
old-gold tiger, draped across my shoulder. No girl
is fully dressed without one.
        Tank Girl
jotted down the next appointment like a child
who'd just learnt to write, while the thick, dark
ink stained my frayed, punk-boy
T-shirt, poked *Tracy loves Darren* with the end
of her pen and winked, "We'll cover him up in no time."

It takes an hour to obliterate girl meets boy,
a minute for childhood to end,
and for dark blue to fade to grey, a lifetime.

SAMANTHA

The soundtrack is Joplin's *Summertime*.
There's a pink calling card: 'Samantha, naughty schoolgirl,
18' and a mobile number. Her East-End
accent sounds younger. "Got a child
of three, another on the way. I think it's a boy
cos it kicks like Beckham." Her lashes flutter long, dark,

rapid as spider's legs. "They can't see my bump in the dark.
I work Stamford Hill mostly. My first time
was 96. We was really broke. Boy
from the local estate. Dealer. The girls
put me up to it. Once I got over the taste it was child's
play. Sucked him like an ice lolly in June. We call it 'making ends

meet.'" Cut to cars pulling up at the rear-end
of the street, headlights stabbing the dark
like words puncturing silence. "Dad's dead. Spoilt me as a child,
everything brand new. Even when he was doing time.
Still miss him. Never loved a man since. I may be a girl
who knows how to give a boy

a good time but I never ever kiss them on the lips. My boy-
friend? The Handsome Pimp. He owns a flat up West End.
Cash. Married with three kids but I'm his no.1 girl."
She's sucking a king-size Silk Cut, dark
shadows where her cheeks should be. "We call half-time
at midnight an' I check on my kid. You can't leave a child

home alone. Pervs. Like my stepdad. I was still a child
when he did it. Told her I was sleeping with boys
but she walked in on us that lunchtime,
and called me a whore. Jealous bitch. I left that weekend.
Fourteen, and still scared of the dark.
Found myself on the streets with the girls."

Close-up black-and-white snapshot of Samantha as a young girl,
smiling. "I'd die if anything happened to my kid. A child
keeps you sane. Takes after her dad. He was dark,
really black. Jamaican. My boy-
friend treats her like she's home-grown. Weekends
at her dad's when I do overtime."

She exhales into the dark, a landlady calling 'Time'
on a bank holiday weekend, then adds, "All men are boys,"
and her unborn child kicks like an underage cancan girl.

LEILA

If she were a time
she'd be midnight, big hand on little, girl
surrendering to womanhood, the fierce end
of needles pointing blood. She's yesterday's child
ticking red ellipses, leaving a trail for boys
to find her. And she controls the dark

as if she were princess of the dark
eclipsing the prince, wrapping a century of time
round her ring finger, making that special boy
wait for that one fine day she'll say "yes". When the girl,
laced tight in the bondage of child-
hood, lets down her braided longing till the end

is moist with dew and her sentence ends
with her lover climbing into the dark,
damp chamber, the witch's brainchild.
And if she were a time
she'd be midnight, twelve black girls
smooching twelve black boys

to the twelve-bar blues, each boy
a prince, girl a princess at the end
of the evening, the last dance, when the girls
trace the licorice lips of the dark
and the stars wink in time
with the bass and the moon is fat with child.

When she who exchanged her necklace, ring and child
for glittering gold must discover the name of the old boy,
the wise man, the wizard. And if she were a time
she'd be midnight, when eternal day ends
and begins in the seamless dark,
the rite of passage from girl

to thirteen. When the bejewelled girl
in cut-glass slippers turns street child,
flinching as each stroke reverberates the dark,
dreaming all night of her shoe-shine boy,
their diamond wedding, that happy end-
ing. If she were a time

she'd be midnight, when each child paints the dark
with fantasy, when girls become women, boys
become men and Once upon a time ... becomes The End.

LABOURERS OF LOVE

THE ART OF CREATION

I

Teardrop in a teat pipette,
my fate lies in the litmus:
pink or blue.

II

My secret garden's in bud but
I can't stand the smell of red roses.

III

All night
I dream of morning sickness.
All day I crave nutritious sleep.

IV

I'm eating crab apples
as if an anaconda
sold them to me.

V

My child shall inherit the earth.
I swallow grains at dusk
sweet with dew.

VI

Baby's treadmilling my belly.
They learn to run before they can walk.

VII

I shall breastfeed.
I shall front crawl myself fit.
I long to see my feet.

VIII

Our first, real conflict.
One of us wants to go out,
the other, to sleep.

IX

My mind, my body
open, a fist unclenching.
Then I hear her cry.

WEIGHTS AND MEASURES AND FINDING A RHYME
FOR ORANGE

*In 1996 American sculptor and concrete poet Carl Andre,
exhibited Sand-Lime Instar, a reincarnation of his controversial
'Tate Bricks', at the Museum of Modern Art, Oxford. I ran three
poetry workshops during the museum's Family Day. This poem is
dedicated to Carl Andre and my workshop participants.*

1983

Oxford is tinted with early Autumn's ginger
as I approach Pembroke Street and change
from Benin Bronze to fresher. Three fat layers,
vest, blouse, home-made sweater and the weight
of a Sainsbury's bag. Tea. Coffee. Poetry.
I'm learning to mark up poetry that rhymes
and discovering a family of feminine half-rhymes:
The Museum of Modern Art (MOMA), pizza and ginger
wine hangover. The symmetry of poetry.
In my mirror I sense the shadows change.
Formal dinner. Late-night bar. The dull weight
of a blackout. Its impenetrable layers.

1987

Poets are similar to bricklayers
except we repeat rhythms or rhymes
instead of bricks, and houses still carry more weight
than poems. I am still attempting to rhyme   orange
with something. Please could you coin some change?
I'm measuring women for M&S. Still write poetry.
An expert on the female form. I figure poetry
is the image of my old college room through two layers
of glass as women strip down to the epidermis. Times change
but if we wait long enough, everything echoes, rhymes.
Winter, Spring. Tangerine, orange.
I am recording data, beginning with height and weight.

1996

FAMOUS	BRICKS	RETAIN	IRONIC	WEIGHT
OXFORD	MUSEUM	HOUSES	FORMAL	POETRY
COILED	RIBBON	SHINES	BRIGHT	BRONZE
CHALKY	BRICKS	SPROUT	DOUBLE	LAYERS
MAKING	SUBTLE	SILENT	VISUAL	RHYMES
SPIRAL	QUEUES	DONATE	SILVER	CHANGE
POETIC	ARTIST	SENSES	PUBLIC	CHANGE
SHARED	WISDOM	AROUND	POETIC	WEIGHT
FAMILY	GROUPS	SCULPT	DOUBLE	RHYMES
CEMENT	SPRUNG	RHYTHM	SENARY	POETRY
WHILST	OXFORD	SUMMER	SPURNS	LAYERS
BEHIND	MIRROR	SHADES	ADORES	BRONZE

On Pembroke Street we change bricks into poetry,
measure women who wear their weight in bulimic layers,
write poetry that rhymes orange with bronze and ginger.

IF

If only I could light up your smile like Oprah,
enrapture your soul like Queen Latifah,
say a little prayer for you like Aretha,
make your caged bird rise and sing like Maya.
If only I could slide back your blind like Cilla,
and know that you just care for me like Nina,
lend wings to love's javelin like Tessa,
make your head turn, heart flip over like Diana.
If only I could spice up your life like Ginger,
add advantage to love like Martina,
set fire to your cigar like Monica,
make fierce erotic·ah like Madonna,
I'd become Uma, Ursula, Ulrika,
your Angela, your Barbra, your Chaka.

MÉNAGE À TROIS

My husband is extremely good-looking
which is why I married him. Mistake number one.
The second was moving to an uptight English
village that has more cows
than people. And the third?
Falling in love

with falling in love.
So I'm wearing a veil of net curtains, looking
like the wife of a *nouveau riche*. His third.
He calls me his 'exotic one'
and refers to the others as 'cows'.
I'm working on my English

but I detest the English
including my husband whom I still love.
'In India they worship cows,
in Ancient Egypt, cats ...' I'm looking
for a poem by Ted Hughes but can't find one.
He's reading *King Richard the Third*

because he's directing *Richard the Third*
for the local am dram. It's so English.
So I'm learning to use the indefinite pronoun, 'one'
and attempting to distinguish need from love.
Lately, I've become the proverbial queen chastising the looking
glass for her crow's feet and whenever I see cows,

I'm reminded of my sagging breasts. I detest cows.
I'm somewhat enamoured of King Richard the Third.
He's repulsive-looking
and English
but has a certain *je ne sais quoi*. One must love
and be loved by someone,

mustn't one?
And in a country where mad cows
are baked and served with batter, true love
is the only palatable alternative. He's the third
son of an aristocrat, quintessentially English,
and in the shade of a horse chestnut, not bad-looking.

So we're having a rendezvous with no-one looking
except for a herd of cows. I adore the English
expression, 'love triangle'. But I wonder who'll come third.

69 BPM

My love's at a delicate frequency
pulsing between lust and envy, seven
inches of raw vinyl emotion with
no gossamer/featherlite protection.

I listen in the foetal position
umbilically connecting with her
as she hits that top note twice in one bar.
My lover is a twelve-digit number

a foreign tongue. Only I can fathom
its syncopated rhythm, postmodern
ménage à trois, she, me, BT. This is
the oral sexual revolution. Love

French kissing at 69 bpm.
The last dance in cheap yellow light. Over
and out. I couldn't hear my heart beat, break.
Too much interference, too much distance.

COUNTDOWN TO ZERO

King Barber
high priest of graffiti
I'm chic as Queen Nefertiti
so sculpt me
some serious old skool lyrics
hieroglyphics
from way back when.
You've got ten minutes.
So get your clippers clipping,
watch time slipping
through our fingers singing auld lang syne.
I wanna haircut so bad they dial 999.
But I don't wanna tempt fate, so wait:
I wanna look like Angela in '68
so make my hair grow,
give me an afro
cos I'm fiercer than Biafra
and blacker than the beetle in Kafka.
Hip 24/7
but I won't go to heaven
with a fade more wicked than 666
so give me a hi-five
get those clippers vibrating
cos the lady is waiting
for the King of the Barbers to start creating
like a rapper riding a 4/4 beat
like it's a wild thing,
you're the style king,
freestyling in 3-D,
about to make me cooler than The Three Degrees
cos you're the MC,
master of clippers,
one two one two,
no.1 of the Wahl crew,
sculptor of my ego,
you cut it down and watch it grow
so be my hero,
take it down
take it down
take it down
to zero.

WHO'S WHO?

1. *Beloved*: Tony Harrison or Toni Morrison?
2. Famous Irish poet: Yeats or Keats?
3. *Puppy Love*: Donny Osmond or Ozzy Osbourne?
4. *Blockbuster*: Sweet or The Beat?
5. *Psycho*: Anthony Perkins or Anthony Hopkins?
6. Passive resistance: Mahatma Gandhi or Muhammad Ali?
7. *Playschool*: Fenella Fielding or Floella Benjamin?
8. *Space Shit*: Chris Ofili or Salvador Dali?
9. *Some Like It Hot*: Marlon Brando or Marilyn Monroe?
10. *She's Gotta Have It*: Mike Leigh or Spike Lee?
11. Pop art: Andy Warhol or Adam Chodzko?
12. *Water Lilies*: Monet or Manet?
13. Scary Spice: Mel B or Mel C?
14. *Bohemian Rhapsody*: Cream or Queen?
15. Split britches: PJ Harvey or PJ Proby?
16. Rowan Atkinson: Mr Benn or Mr Bean?
17. *The Flea*: Thom Gunn or John Donne?
18. *Frankenstein*: Mary Kenney or Mary Shelley?
19. Del Boy: James Mason or David Jason?
20. *School Days*: Nick Berry or Chuck Berry?
21. Rock dinosaur: Cliff Richard or Keith Richards?
22. *Zorba the Greek*: Anthony Quinn or Anthony Quayle?
23. *Misunderstanding*: Genesis or Oasis?
24. *He's a Rebel*: The Crystals or Crystal Gayle?
25. *Rebel Of The Underground*: Tupak Shakur or Kula Shaker?
26. *The Artist*: CK Williams or William Carlos Williams?
27. *Other Lovers*: Jackie Kay or Cathy Acker?
28. *Prime Suspect*: Helen Mirren or Karen Millen?
29. *GBH*: Robert Lindsay or Albert Finney?
30. *Best Of My Love*: The Beatles or The Eagles?
31. *Myra*: Marcus Garvey or Marcus Harvey?
32. Composer: Engelbert Humperdinck or Engels?
33. *To Celia*: Ben Jonson or Dr Johnson?
34. *How Deep Is Your Love?* The Three Degrees or The Bee Gees?
35. *Death Wish*: Charles Bronson or Charles Manson?
36. *Bring Tha Noize*: Public Image or Public Enemy?
37. *Call Up The Groups*: The Barron Knights or Barry White?
38. *Red Light Spells Danger*: Phil Oakey or Billy Ocean?
39. *It's In His Kiss*: Cher or Shere Hite?
40. Poet Laureate: Andrew Marr or Andrew Motion?

MOTHERS OF INVERSION

THE CHANGE

I remember everything vividly that Sunday
by its absence. It was the day that God,
like Father Christmas and the tooth fairy,
no longer existed. The church smelt musty
and I noticed Mrs Leadbetter's glass eye.
I remember lip synching the Lord's Prayer

and Amen after father murmured grace
for Sunday dinner. At the head of the table
sat a leg of lamb, more like a sacrifice
than a roast. Our golden Labrador, Petra,
sloped off into the sitting room, and hid.

Father carved while mother served raw carrots,
pureed swede and something resembling cabbage.
I can still taste it in the back of my throat.
The only sound was stainless steel on china

till I realised the potatoes were missing
and said it, and my mother turned, a blur
of plate spinning across the room and breaking.

My father said "She's going through The Change".
I stared into the kitchen floor and wondered

what, in God's name, she was changing into.

AJAX

Part I. Parallel Lines

Just spent my last tenner on white powder, trading
Charles Dickens' crumpled face for a fading

pink postage-stamp envelope sealed with a loving kiss.
Supply and demand = business.

OPEN SESAME

Parallel lines deck my mirror,
my destiny mapped out by razor

blade, destination North South
in through the nose, out through the mouth

and it's that ski-jump Winter Olympics 78 kick
time is flitting, flying, and it's magic.

My pupils shrink to a full stop, minute,
my nostrils sprint and my mouth, mute

with soap begins its terrible grinding
dance and I swallow hard like it's a double brandy lining

the inside of the glass like stretch satin.
And I'm Alice, Ali Baba, Aladdin

in the fast lane on the fast stuff.
Don't stop till you get enough.

Time streaks on roller skates faster than a double-decker bus
down streets decked with disco lights, paved with gold dust
to The Underground, the whizz kid's placenta
for the bright lights of the city centre.

OPEN SESAME

Part II. Fly The Tube

I'm devouring the sad ads on the Northbound
till I choke on PENALTY FARE £10

and study the facades on the opposite seat
Trainspotting, *Crash* and *Deadmeat*.

'Fly the Tube', I'd rather take a plane
Concorde, to be exact, high on cocaine

'High as a feather boa
70s fashion victim strangles tube controller

for going too slow.' That's my mind
working overtime, nose to the grind

and the wages of snorting class ABCs?
a) calcium deficiency
b) warped reality
c) split personality

OPEN SESAME

Typical that the doors of perception are jammed
when the queen of the star-studded dance floor's in demand.

Time pauses meaningfully, mean
then doors part and time fast forwards, clean
up the down escalator and run
jumps the queue at Club 2001.

OPEN SESAME

Part III. Do What You Wanna Do

They call me Jax, though my real name's Eva
the whole of the Jackson Five rolled into one serious diva

No.1 on the guest list, top of the charts
when I make my grand entrance, the sea of sequins parts.

They're playing Do What You Wanna Do, my cue
cos a girl's gotta do what a girl's gotta do

Do The Hustle, Le Freak, says Chic,
Shake your body down to the ground. Then peak.

90s out, 70s in
dance till our bodies Siamese twin.

I take a mammoth dab of uncut paranoia.
Now I won't speak without a lawyer

and they're playing *Night fever night fever*
from the best disco album in the world, ever

yeah, the Bee Gees are the bee's knees, honey,
now there goes a man who turns drugs into money

but not tonight, I'm skint and sky high
and on a scale from 'disco' to 'psycho'
I'm 'get out of my fucking space or die'.

Time pulsates at 100 BPM
into the small hours of REM
and the contracted pupils of the chemical class
need to download for the last dance.

OPEN SESAME

Part IV. The Sweet Shop

Open secret. Most of this loo queue have succumbed
to downing uppers, down-in-ones,

don't-look-in-the-mirrors and don't-stop-
till-you-get-enoughs. Welcome to the sweet shop

where white light overexposes shady deals
and crisp tenners convert to cheap thrills.

OPEN SESAME

Toilet lid down, the dregs, a thin white line
lines my nostril and drug-fucked I'm bleached clean,
cloned, confused, fused. 5:59.

OPEN SESAME

Time: 6am Time to unpick
sleep stitched lids. Time to get rich quick
or just get by. Aja, family lawyer from Nigeria,
leaves for her two-pounds-an-hour job as cleaner.

Part V. One-Way Ticket

6am Now 70s chic looks cheap
as I boogie oogie oogie to the beep beep beep

of a space invader machine, worn-out, wide-eyed
my chewing gum long-spun and tumble-dried,

an item of off-white laundry. Time to exit.
Bright light. Day breaks my spirit.

Time: 6:30am Aja scans the tube ads, prays.
For only God the omnipotent can raise
her spirits in this London, her sugar cane
dreams drowned, choked by cisterns and chains.

OPEN SESAME

I watch her ascent as I'm coming down
and midway, in this split second, we common ground,

merge, parallel lines, North South, split
personalities, converge, compound, commit.

One-way ticket. That's the way I like it.

DOUBLE ENTENDRE

I

Soho, London. The sky a true blue lit by a mellow yellow sun. It's pay day. Tomorrow's May Day. Bread heads and scene queens shop till they drop. Greed meets need. Toy boys clutch mobile phones, high fliers dive underground, and doppelgängers hit Clone Zone. The air is fish and chips and vinegar and lager, the hustle and bustle condensed to hubbub.

Tia Maria enters the pub, orders dry white wine. There's Bizzy Lizzy the speed freak, a hippy chick talking poppycock, a fat cat, a fag hag and gender-bender rubber stuffer Handy Andy.

"Tia Maria," he cries, hitting *My Girl* on the juke box, "A blast from the past!" and he's lip synching. Someone hit the trip switch, please.

"Andy!" she replies, wide-eyed and pierced eared, "How are you?"

"Solo. The shit hit the fan. She was sex on legs in long johns but wore pritt-stick for lipstick," he replies. "And how are uhu?"

"OK," she says, "It's payday. Let's spend spend spend. What's it to be?"

"Double G&T, girl. It's prime time."

Happy hour in slo-mo. The end of a lazy hazy day. What's it to be? Crush the rumble in the jungle with some pub grub. Eat to the beat. Hip-hop, cock-rock, rub-a-dub-dub. Double this, double that. Down in one. Rhubarb rhubarb, yak yak, blah blah blah.

"Cheers. Here's to life."

They clink drinks, once, twice, hit a note so high that they clash, smash like a windscreen in a car crash. Like Brixton and Brick Lane, the Soho streets are paved with broken glass.

Amstel, Amsterdam. The sky a true blue lit by an old gold sun. It's Queen's Day. Scene queens and dykes on bykes shop till they drop. Brits go Dutch. Toy boys clutch mobile phones, high fliers take the glam tram, and drunken pals hit the canals. The air is satay on chips and orange liquor, the whole city set to binge on orange things.

Café au Lait enters the coffee shop, orders scotch on the rocks, lights a joint. There's Fuzzy Wuzzy and the Hair Bear Bunch, Smokey Joe, Annie the Tranny aka The Floozy in the Jacuzzi and gender-bender *fille de nuit* Neon Dionne.

"Café au Lait!" she screams, hitting *My Guy* on the juke box, "A blast from the past!" and she's lip synching. Someone hit the trip switch, please.

"Dionne!" replies Café au Lait, sucking hard on her home grown, "How are you?"

"Solo. The shit hit the fanny. He was sex on legs in PVC but wore wheels of steel in his conga eel," she replies. "And how are you, go-go girl? Still selling your cunny for money?"

"Yeah, you gotta writhe to survive. And it's Queen's day. Let's spend spend spend. What's it to be?"

"A Between the Sheets, if you please."

A happy hour in slo-mo. What's it to be? Space cake or pass the dutchie get the munchies? Eat to the beat. Hip-hop, cock-rock, rub-a-dub-dub. Double, double, no toil, no trouble. Down in one, jabber jabber, blah blah blah.

"Proost!"

They clink drinks, once, twice, in their mind's eye see their inner-city web where neon streets and coffee shops meet. Where red lights spotlight shop windows and they, black widows, spin sugar candy seduction. Like jet set in perspex, their dual fates are sealed in low-cut glass.

CLAWS

Hans was left-handed as in *Mano Destra* but preferred action
    adventures to arty farties.
She wore tan leather brogues and second-hand clothes, crisp shirts
    and tailor-made suits from the 30s and 40s.
Being big, black and butch and hard as nails with a heart of gold
    gave Hans a pulling advantage
for if fingers be green and dykes be wine then Hans was bubbly,
    true East London vintage.

Hans was left-handed, and was her handshake firm? I'd say oui,
    I'd say si, I'd say yes, I'd say ja.
She intimidated both boys and men but attracted women and girls
    like *It Could Be You*:
women travelled by cab from North and South in long satin
    gloves, in dresses of satin and chintz;
in their Sunday best from East and West, girls would sharpen their
    claws if they thought they were in with a chance.

Hans was left-handed, more left side of the brain than right, more
    matter-of-fact than fiction.
Twice a week she shaved her hair and filed her nails to nought
    seeking 1-2-1 affection.
Wanda was a famous beautician, a lifeline for hundreds of
    glamourous East End women,
an archetypal Cancer, with a Scorpio rising, seeking the perfect
    woman.

Hans was left-handed, smoked cigars, drank cognac chasers, a
    butch dyke through and through.
Hans liked her women forward, femme and fun to be with, and
    Wanda was all three.
"I can manicure, I can pedicure, but the ultimate cure is the one
    that I won't be selling.
I can read your palm, I can read your mind, so meet me 1.30,
    Saturday, in my salon."

Hans was left-handed and once paid cash to have both hands
  prettily painted with henna
but that was then and this is now, for this is Hans and that, shall
  we say, was Hannah
yet she found herself outside *Hollywood Nails*, with sweaty palms,
  and it is no wonder
for if ever a woman could wrap Hans round her incy-wincy finger,
  it was Wanda.

Hans was left-handed and kept her left intact but surrendered her
  right to each nail extension,
to Wanda's gentle, magic touch, till Hans' pure butch persona
  faced extinction
till the watchful minute and second hands had each performed
  their final revolution,
till Hans had claws more predatory than any beast in the Book
  of Revelation.

Hans was left-handed, a fortune teller once read her palm and
  calmly predicted quins
and the fruit of Wanda's manual labour far outshone the drag of
  a thousand queens
and Hans felt like Edward Scissorhands, The Hammer House of
  Horror hand that haunted,
emasculated, emancipated, dressed to kill, the hunter and the
  hunted.

THE STING

At twelve I learnt about The Fall,
had rough-cut daydreams based on original sin,
nightmares about the swarm of thin-
lipped, foul-mouthed, crab apple-
masticating girls who'd chase me full
throttle: me, slipping on wet leaves, a heroine
in a black-and-white cliché; them, buzzing on nicotine
and the sap of French kisses. I hated big school
but even more, I hated the lurid shame
of surrender, the yellow miniskirt
my mother wore the day that that man
drove my dad's car to collect me. She called my name
softly, more seductive than an advert.
I heard the drone of the engine, turned and ran.

THE SHIFT

He used to finish off her sentences
and buy her clothes that labelled her the wife
of a director. Both the cars were his.
He'd drink whisky as an aperitif,
and pat his belly as if he'd given birth
to four fine sons. Until the hour
they called her from that hospital up North
and she drove three hundred miles in second gear.

She mows the lawn now, uproots weeds like the whiskers
that dominate her chin, wears shapeless slacks,
translates his faint, infantile gestures
into cups of tea and sandwiches, and smokes
Golden Virginia. When he goes, she'll curse
the stiff confinement of her one, black dress.

TRANSFORMATRIX

I'm slim as a silver stiletto, lit
by a fat, waxing moon and a seance
of candles dipped in oil of frankincense.
Salt peppers my lips as the door clicks shut.
A pen poised over a blank page, I wait
for madam's orders, her strict consonants
and the spaces between words, the silence.
She's given me a safe word, a red light
but I'm breaking the law, on a death wish,
ink throbbing my temples, each vertebra
straining for her fingers. She trusses up
words, lines, as a corset disciplines flesh.
Without her, I'm nothing but without me
she's tense, uptight, rigid as a full stop.